New Dad at 40

A VERY SHORT BOOK OF ESSENTIALS
TO GET YOU THROUGH PREGNANCY
AND THE FIRST YEAR.

by Aaron Charles Sylvan

Published by Lemonade Press
Sylvan Social Technology, LLC
534 Third Avenue, Suite 1248
Brooklyn, NY 11215

Front cover design by Aaron Charles Sylvan
Front cover typefaces are Swashington and Arca Moderna.
Interior text is set in Adobe Caslon Pro.
Illustrations by Fiverr artist GraphicHarvest.
Thanks to dads Jeff Williams, Chad Lembree, and Ben Weiss.
Very special thanks to M. M. DeVoe, for her tremendous guidance.

PRINT ISBN-13: 978-0-9914548-4-6
EBOOK ISBN-13: 978-0-9914548-5-3

Printed in the United States of America

For Brandon

After I became a Dad, you were my first friend to announce an expected child. Your news inspired me to share the lessons learned on my journey.

Contents

Contents i

Inclusivity Preface vii

Introduction 1

    Unpaid Endorsements   2

    Getting Ready   2

Common Daddy Fears 3

    "I won't get to hang out at the bar any more"   3

    "I won't be able to afford what my kid needs"   3

    "I feel weird around kids"   5

    "I never understand what kids are saying"   6

    "I can't stand kids' TV or movies"   7

    "I'll lose all my friends"   7

    "People say I'll never get to sleep again"   7

Pregnancy Shopping List 8

    Month 5: Big Furniture   8

Month 6: Babymoon   *9*

Month 7: Big Accessories   *10*

Month 8: Baby Shower   *11*

Month 9: Baby Registry   *11*

So What Is All This Crap?..**13**

Glider   *13*

Bassinet   *14*

Baby Björn   *15*

Strollers (What the Types Are)   *16*

Strollers (So What Do I Buy?)   *20*

Other Important Stuff   *21*

Feeding...**31**

Nursing   *31*

Formula   *32*

Bottles   *32*

Breast Pump   *33*

Alcohol   *34*

Brands...**35**

Stores   *35*

Clothes & Linens   *35*

Accessories 36

Shipping 36

Local Stores 37

The Hospital Trip **38**

Pick a Hospital Soon 38

Pick a Pediatrician, Too 39

Bring to Hospital 40

Camera in Hospital 40

Delivery Date 41

Epidural 41

Learning Diapers, Swaddling, Bottle 42

Weird Dots and Spots 43

Stock Up 43

Tax, Tag, and Title 44

Start College Savings Right Away 44

First Days Home **46**

The Good News 46

The Bad News 46

Consequences 47

How to Eat 47

How to Stay Sane   48

They Sleep A Lot   49

Tons of Pictures & Videos   49

Daddy Pics   50

First Date & Date Nights   51

Parental Leave from Work   52

The First Year **54**

Your New Community   54

Bubble   55

Quiet or Loud House   55

Social Media   56

Passwords   57

Day Care   57

Sign Language   58

Pacifier   58

Weaning   58

Sleep **59**

Co-Sleeping   59

Sleep Training — Quick Summary   60

First Birthday   61

Sleep Training: A Deeper Dive..............................63

    "Cry It Out"   64

    "Ferberizing"   64

    "Cave in"   64

Other Books 67

    Reference   67

    Humor   68

Things to Look Forward To..............................69

Conclusion 70

Inclusivity Preface

Love can take many forms, and I respect them all.

Throughout this book, my language assumes you're a man, married to a woman who is pregnant or recently gave birth. I write conversationally, from my own experiences.

Obviously some parts, such as labor, delivery, and nursing, are specific to reproductive biology.

However, 90% of this book is equally appropriate regardless of marital status, adoption, gender identity, sexual orientation, or any other categorizations of domestic partners.

No matter who you are, I wish your child may grow up in a world more universally welcoming than ours is today.

Introduction

#1: "You got this." If you're sweating, don't.

You are about to have the adventure of a lifetime — *literally* — because you are about to create the adventure that is someone else's life!

The bad news about being out of your 20s: No lie, there are some challenges in being an older dad. Kids are energetic, and you might find it hard to keep up, or to get down on the floor as much as they like. You might be in your 60s for their graduation ceremonies, or have people call you "grandpa" when you visit at school. Bummer.

The great news about being out of your 20s: Your emotions are more grounded. What you lack in energy, you make up for in wisdom. Your finances are more stable (even if you're not as rich as you might hope, at least you know where you stand.) Perhaps you have some more freedom in your work environment, such as better control over your schedule than when you were younger.

As someone who spent many of my years single, and who never felt like a "baby person", I was very surprised by the parenting adventure. I was afraid that maybe I wouldn't be a natural Dad or be comfortable with my child. Fortunately, those fears disappeared — literally the moment she was born.

But during the pre-arrival preparations, and throughout the First Year, I learned a lot. We did some things right, many things wrong, and I spent a ton of time researching and buying products of all kinds.

Unpaid Endorsements

In this book, I recommend quite a few products. I have not been paid by any of those companies, and I am not using any kind of "tracking links" or generating affiliate sales revenue in any way. It's just a list of products I liked.

Getting Ready

Since your baby hasn't arrived yet, you still have time to prepare. When baby gets home, you will be overwhelmed. It will be easier if you have a complete set of "starter supplies" already purchased and set up in your house somewhere.

You can save yourself a bunch of trouble by buying some of the right supplies *now*. Even if it's only the second trimester, it's good to get the big stuff out of the way. (Expectant mommies with big bellies aren't good at taking long trips through parking lots and superstores, and there are decisions she won't want to be left out of.)

The "you really want this" shopping list comes to about $2,000-3,000. (You can do the house furniture for $900, appliances like stroller and carriers for $700, and the "getting baby home from hospital kit" for $400.) Obviously you can also double the cost of everything. I think it's more important to *have* every item on this list, than to have "the best" of every item on the list.

But before the shopping, let's first address some of your likely concerns:

Common Daddy Fears

"I won't get to hang out at the bar any more"

ANSWER: You're in your 40s; you had your time to hang out in bars and nightclubs and all that. Remember when you were young, and sometimes there would be an older person in the corner, making you wonder "Why is that creep hanging out here and looking at us?" Don't be that creep.

Listen, you can still meet your friends sometimes — it just won't be as often, and you won't get sloshed any more. Which is probably where you should be these days, anyway. If you used to go out once a week, it might get dialed back to once a month. If it used to be once a month, maybe now it's once every few months. But the first time you wake up hung over with your kid looking you in the eye at 6am and wanting you to be cheerful… you're going to feel pretty small. Hopefully you won't do it a second time.

"I won't be able to afford what my kid needs"

ANSWER: Well, if you're thinking about the tens or hundreds of thousands of dollars over your child's lifetime, then maybe you're right. But before you freak out too hard, let's just worry about the first few weeks and months.

Newborns don't actually *need* very much. A bunch of changes of clothes, food, diapers and wipes. Mostly they need you. A month's supply of infant food costs less than one nice date night for you and your wife; the same for diapers.

Start thinking about your home. If you live in a big city, you might not have a spare bedroom for your baby. Start seriously considering doing whatever it takes to make that happen (even if it means moving someplace more remote). Baby is pretty immobile for the first 6 months, so "childproofing" is not an immediate necessity. But by the time your child can crawl, make sure your home is appropriate.

Education can be expensive, but it's years away. Let's break it down, so you can think about specifics instead of just carrying blank fear: A four-year private college education today can cost more than a quarter million dollars, so you might start saving soon (but it's not a concern for you *this year*). K-12 education at a top private school can be as much as $600,000 (less for religion-affiliated schools), but again, that doesn't start for more than five years.

If you don't have a cool extra mil sitting around for grade school plus college education, expect to do what everyone else does: consider moving to a good public school district, and start saving for college ASAP.

For higher education, remember that State Universities are cheaper and loans are available, and also that the entire cost structure of college could change between now and when your child is ready to enroll.

For K-12, many public schools determine where your child can go to kindergarten based on your home address around age 5. Which means you have time. *None of this matters right now, so first focus on the short term.*

Day Care cost is significant. If you and your wife work, then day care or a nanny will be a significant expense. Expect $2,000-3,000/month if you live in or near a big city. Maybe half that in modest suburbs. Also that price is for a "full day", which is code for "9am-3pm". If you actually plan to work a regular job, then you'll need to pay the day care for "extended stay", which normally means 6pm.

In some areas, spaces at good day cares are limited and fill years in advance, so if your wife is more than 3 months pregnant then it's quite reasonable to start looking now, and maybe getting onto waiting lists. Remember, it's usually free or near-free to be on a wait list.

You can save money by doing a "nanny share" or some kind of co-op, where groups of parents either take turns or just split the cost of one caregiver... but if you can afford day care, little kids benefit from spending the day with each other.

Formally organized and licensed programs are more likely to have teachers (yes, they call them "teachers" even for infants) with formal education in Early Childhood.

Plus, even if you can afford time away from work, it's exhausting, especially at your age, trying to keep a tiny one stimulated. Day cares will offer all kinds of things that you won't have the time or patience for, like playing in colored water or sand or glitter or other things that probably aren't in your house.

"I feel weird around kids"

ANSWER: You mean, "What if I don't bond with my kid and he or she just seems like a weird drooling pooping alien, and I don't feel the way I'm supposed to feel?" Don't worry, this will not happen. Because biology.

"I never understand what kids are saying"

ANSWER: Yes, it can be awkward. But here's the deal: Before age 2 they don't say much at all. Around age 2-3, they can speak in a way that probably only their parents understand. And not so well. I won't lie, this phase is sometimes tough.

But after a few years of hearing nothing, it's pretty damn exciting recognizing even just a word or two. It's fun learning how to understand them. And they get super-excited that they're able to express themselves, so you'll be sharing the joy. By age 3-4, they should start speaking clearly enough that even other people can understand your kids. (Or you'll "translate".)

Plus sometimes they do cool stuff like give random people the finger. You will get a new idea of what's funny.

"I can't stand kids' TV or movies"

ANSWER: It's not all as bad as you think. True, some children's television is horrendous. But remember, it's created by grown-ups. Some of them understand that other grown-ups have to watch it... and they bury clever grown-up humor, or references to pop movies and music from when you were a kid, and so on.

"I'll lose all my friends"

ANSWER: Well, you may lose a few, especially the dedicated partiers. But you will make new ones, who will share your new interests. In our case, after our daughter was born we made far more friends than in the fifteen years before.

The playgrounds and birthday parties and events are not as bad as you think. Remember again, you can hang out with the other parents. Commiserate. Some kids' parties even have grown-up drinks. Also, kids have like zero attention span... so a "giant party" might mean 30 minutes of running around and then 30 minutes of pizza. All done! You can handle it.

"People say I'll never get to sleep again"

ANSWER: The struggle is real.

Pregnancy Shopping List

Don't wait for Baby to be born. Do these things right away.

Month 5: Big Furniture

Buy early because furniture delivery can take months, and delays are common. You'll be pissed if the baby arrives and you still have noplace but your dining table for changing diapers.

$300+ Glider Chair
$400+ Changing Table / Dresser
$200+ Crib

You can do the key furniture items for $1000. (Or more if you like, but most of these aren't lifetime investments.)

Absolutely unconditionally you must do the glider, even if you blow off the other items. Someone in your house will be feeding your baby in the middle of the night. It's comfortable and relaxing to do this while gently rocking in a chair, but it's exhausting to do while standing.

During the first two years, you and your partner will spend a lot of time carrying 8, 10, even 20 pounds of added weight… being able to lean back and take a load off your feet is an opportunity to bring bliss to your life. Indeed, this purchase may be the most beloved item in our entire house.

Since it's a place where people sleep, consider one with "wings" on the back for resting your head.

Month 6: Babymoon

Regardless of the size or budget, make sure you do something special.

Plan a trip, as late as she can comfortably travel (probably Month 6 or so). It's okay for Mommy to fly (always ask a doctor this stuff; your pregnancy may be different). But if a doctor says it is safe, do something relaxing and romantic. *This will be literally the last time you travel as non-parents.* Once your kid is born, you might take a trip while baby is with grandparents or somesuch, but you will still *be* parents. That never ends, obvs.

Take some pics showing off the baby bump (even though it may still be small). Pro Tip: When you make the hotel reservation, in the "notes" field you can make requests like, "When we arrive, please surprise us with a cheese plate immediately." Or freshly-cut fruit. Try asking for chocolate-covered strawberries if the place seems fancy enough to handle that. Have them bring two glasses of champagne, even!

No, one single glass of bubbly a month won't destroy your kid. Oh, but do be careful about letting random people see Mommy enjoy her one glass, since some folks will freak out and get all judgey. Especially because they assume it's "not just one". And more especially because they need to STFU and mind their own business. But really, this "one last trip" can be very special. Plan whatever you can.

We're from New York, and we're not dripping in money... so for us an affordable romantic winter getaway was 3 days at a romantic hotel in Florida. (I think we found discount airfare for $200/person roundtrip, and hotels are moderately priced). You don't need to charter a private jet to Necker Island. Just do *something* because it will be a cherished memory.

Don't wait much past 6 months for a Babymoon, because soon Mommy will have trouble with seat belts, luggage, walking around, etc.

Month 7: Big Accessories

Shop for these with Mommy. They'll be a big part of your life for the next few years, so she will want to have a say in the process. *Don't wait until Month 9, because then Mommy might no longer have the energy for shopping.*

- Stroller ($250-900)
- Bassinet ($30-300)
- Car Seat ($100-400)
- On-Body Carrier (Björn/K'tan) ($150/$50)
- Changing Pad ($100)
- Diaper Bag ($50-200)

Total cost for these vitals can be around $700, although you can triple that if you like spending. More on these specific items later. Don't worry. I've got ya.

Month 8: Baby Shower

It's traditional to do this as late as possible, when Mommy looks like she's going to pop. But in Month 9 she may have difficulty getting around. Plus babies sometimes arrive early. So probably do this at the beginning of Month 9. If you can, hand this over to a group of women. If not, you can do it yourself. Invite her friends, especially those who are already mothers.

Set up a registry on Amazon or somesuch, for the "month 9 items". A week after the party, buy everything else on the list. Ideally, this party is for women/mothers only. Even you should piss off. Maybe help with setup and cleanup, or join for the final 30 minutes to show your support. But this is an important opportunity for your wife to talk with other women about things like breastfeeding, vaginal tearing, weight gain, stretch marks, libido... and I *promise* you she'll feel more comfortable if there are no men in the room. And so will you.

Month 9: Baby Registry

People will want to buy you things. If you're in a high income bracket, there's no shortage of companies with pricey offerings — you don't need help choosing silver spoons, picture frames, cashmere, etc. Think "Tiffany".

If you are very comfortable financially, you'll be just fine with zero prep, going to local stores or ordering from <u>amazon.com</u> and <u>diapers.com</u> as needed. You don't "need" any of this stuff to be in your house before baby arrives.

However, if you're the kind of person who likes to be prepared… or if you're concerned with family expenses (no shame there), you might put these items onto a Gift Registry for the Baby Shower. Then you only need to buy only what is left over.

- ☑ Desitin — $6
- ☑ A&D Ointment — $6
- ☑ Wipes for newborn — $26
- ☑ Diapers (size "newborn", duh) — $28
- ☑ Chux (disposable pads) — $14
- ☑ First bath supplies — $28
- ☑ Diaper Genie — $34
- ☑ Snot Sucker — $4
- ☑ Baby Calendar — $10
- ☑ Bouncy Seat — $20
- ☑ Boppy Pillow — $30
- ☑ Really soft cloths — $9
- ☑ Onesies — $10
- ☑ Receiving Blankets — $22
- ☑ Portable Changing Mat — $24
- ☑ Digital Thermometer — $40
- ☑ Shusher — $40
- ☑ Noise Machine — $99
- ☑ Night Lights — $2 (I like ones that cycle colors)
- ☑ Manhattan Toy — $10 (for teething/gripping)

Around $400 - if you can do it, buy everything on this list. Maybe only one noise machine if money's tight. I'm trying to save you a few freakouts and 4am trips to the 24-hr pharmacy, or painful days waiting for an Amazon delivery, when you could have been spending that time getting much-needed rest.

So What Is All This Crap?

Some of the new additions to your house might be unfamiliar, so here's an abbreviated "new Daddy equipment glossary". BTW, if you think you "don't have room" in your home, you're wrong. You need this stuff, and I promise it will be much easier for you to find a place before the baby arrives. Get on it!

Glider

It's a magic chair. You must get one of these. No kidding. Can easily be done for $300-400. There are some cheap options on wayfair.com, and a wide range at potterybarnkids.com. Or you can spend over $1000 at ethanallen.com, if that's more your budget. But remember that baby will drip milk/formula/fluids on it, so don't get a used glider. Because Eeeew.

The chair is important because babies spend a lot of time with a bottle (or a breast) in their mouth. They can eat in their sleep, and when your baby is being fed at 3am, whoever's doing the feeding might want to be asleep too.

Rocking is one of the best ways to get babies to fall asleep, and they like to be "on you" a lot. Which means that either you can sit in one of these chairs and be super-comfortable, or you can stand and rock your baby for hours until your legs and arms want to fall off. Trust me on this one; the glider is delightful. And mandatory. Quite a few times we have thought it was literally the best $400 we ever spent on anything.

Bassinet

For the first 3 months, baby wants to sleep in a kinda tiny box. We bought an expensive one, and it was totally stupid. (A) Baby doesn't care, and (B) Those three months will vanish in the blink of an eye, and you'll be stuck with something you can't really sell. Google "Moses bassinet" and you'll see options from $30-$300. I promise your baby won't know the difference. Or, your baby's preferences are random and unrelated to price.

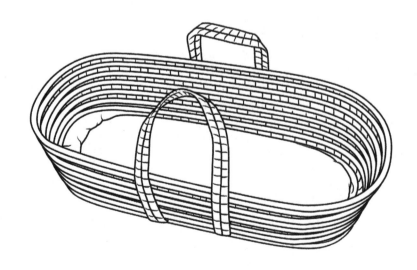

Key Learning: **Anything you buy might have to be replaced because baby simply hates it for no apparent reason.** This is a theme; expect to see it happen a lot more.

We bought the "Halo Bassinest" because we thought its "unique peek-thru mesh" would be nice for us... but in fact the mesh kept baby from sleeping. (Babies get distracted when they can see things, especially their parents.) And we thought the "built-in vibration and lullaby" was clever, but it was like $1 worth of the chintziest electronics imaginable, and it made no difference.

Newborns don't appreciate expensive things. They like being stuffed into a box where things are dark and there's nothing to look at. Remember, they spent the previous 9 months like that.

Baby Björn

There are many kinds of these things. It's like a backwards backpack for carrying your baby on your chest. In general, they're awesome. I was super-squeamish about babies before having my own, but trust me, that disappears instantly after baby arrives. They will occasionally vomit or spit up on you, but that shouldn't affect your decisions. (And if your child hasn't got a health problem, this stuff is honestly quite rare.) You will spend a *lot* of time walking around with baby in your arms. Having a carrier like this means you get the use of your arms back, which is a super-big deal.

The "Björn" brand makes quality products. I'd suggest looking at a few different ones, if you can find a store that will let you try them on. Your first guesses may be wrong; you might buy some stuff and hate it, throw it out and try something else. Super-difficult to predict, so just take a guess and move on.

Just be sure you have something like this in your house from Day 1, even if maybe it's not the right product at first. There are some companies that make sash-like carriers for newborns... "Baby K'tan" is popular, at $59.   As baby changes size, and becomes more or less restless, some of these options get better or worse.   You and your partner should each have your own carrier if you can afford to own two, since adjusting the size can be annoying.

Strollers (What the Types Are)

There are 3 kinds of strollers. "full-sized", "hybrid", and "umbrella". Find the biggest store you can, because you want a wide selection. Get help from a salesperson, and have them show you how to open/collapse the products you're looking at.

Huge Stroller

We were dumb enough to think "more money = automatically better". Two of today's leading brands are "Uppababy" and "Bugaboo", and they're quality products... but regardless of what you can afford, make sure your decisions match your needs. Evaluating the full-sized (huge) strollers:

- PLUS: Very smooth ride over bumps, and rough terrain, which means easier for baby to sleep. These do much better on snow or gravel, too.

- BIG PLUS: You can usually drive them with one hand, which means you can hold a beverage or a phone in the other hand.

- MINUS: But also very hard to lift or fold.

- BIG MINUS: Sometimes too wide for aisles in narrow stores, especially in crowded cities. Your family's primary caregiver will sometimes want to shop in stores or get coffee while baby is sleeping in the stroller, so if you only have one product it shouldn't be this one.

One of these will definitely last until baby outgrows having a stroller - even if you have a second child. The better ones have the important features of letting you (A) snap in a car seat, to transfer sleeping baby from car ↔ stroller, (B) change whether baby is facing backwards to look at parents or facing forwards at outside world. However, weighing something like 25 pounds, you wouldn't take this up or down stairs onto public transportation.

Remember that Mommy is probably less muscular than you, and she will spend the first few months recovering from the trauma of childbirth (including literally cutting or tearing her flesh). Big strollers can be nice, but be sensitive to what she can lift — especially into the trunk of a car.

Hybrid Stroller

Some "middle-of-the-road" strollers are available in the $200-500 price range, with pretty nice ones around $350. I suspect we might have done just fine with one of these, rather than going nuts for the priciest thing we could find (and can now barely lift or fit through the aisles of a tight store).

If you get a stroller that does not have a "bassinet attachment", make sure you ask how old the baby needs to be. Newborns need to lie flat. Also, they're bundled up like a little meatloaf, which means they can't be secured with a strap between their legs. The people in the store will explain this all to you.

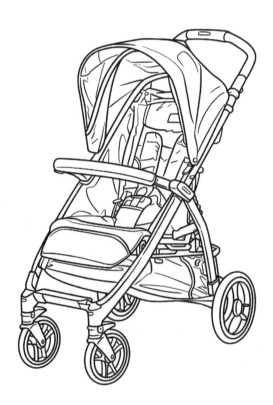

Umbrella Stroller

On the other hand, the "umbrella strollers" fold up like an umbrella (well, maybe the world's most awkward and annoying umbrella), and weigh a lot less than the larger strollers.

Ours is 7 pounds. Baby needs to be bigger (maybe 12-18 months) before riding in one of these, because they need to hold up their head and sit up straight. You won't need an umbrella stroller for a long time. Don't buy this until later.

The tiny wheels guarantee a very loud and bumpy ride - a few times I even launched my kid onto the sidewalk because the stroller hit a tiny bump in the sidewalk and stopped abruptly. (Yes, that's why you should always clip in the straps even when it seems unnecessary...)

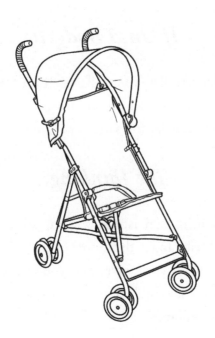

What I hated most about the umbrella stroller is that you always need both hands for pushing, so you can forget about your phone or coffee. But I digress; this isn't part of Year 1.

Strollers (So What Do I Buy?)

If Money no Object:

• Large Stroller with Clip-In Car Seat. And splurge for the Bassinet Attachment (even though it only lasts 3-4 months).
• On-Body Carrier (Björn or K'tan or other) for each parent

If On A Budget:

• Mid-sized "regular" stroller (you won't use it for the first few months)
• Cheapest car seat that you feel you can trust
• One nice On-Body Carrier for parents to share

The Thinking:

For the first 3-4 months, baby isn't strong enough to hold up his/her head, which means you need baby to lay flat. Some of the pricey ones let you snap in a bassinet (baby bed), but it costs extra and you'll throw it out after 90-120 days. Some might have a "lay-flat" option for this purpose, too. **A carrier (like Björn) you can use immediately.**

If you can afford a lie-flat stroller so you can take a walk with your newborn without having to carry your baby in your arms, you'll thank yourself. But if money's tight then don't worry - the time passes quickly and soon any stroller will be fine. Whether you buy a mid-range "hybrid" or a giant high-end stroller, I strongly recommend making the purchase before baby arrives. Also, make sure it has a cup holder (sounds silly, but your hands will be full)! A place for storing stuff underneath is very nice too (such as your diaper bag).

Don't worry about getting "the right size" or "which one baby will like", because baby will have no opinion on this. Once baby arrives, however, you will be too busy for shopping. Get this out of the way.

Other Important Stuff

Car Seat

In NYC, the hospital won't let you drive your baby home unless you show that you have a car seat and know how to use it. (This is a law.) I dunno about other states, but if you have a car and you drive, then you obviously need a car seat. Install it at least a week before baby's due date. Don't take much help from others on the installation, either, since it's kind of a nuisance and you need to be comfortable doing it yourself. Let someone show you the proper installation, and practice until you can do it yourself.

Pretty much all cars have special super-sturdy brackets hidden in the back seat, which are very safe (jam your hand deep into the area where the seat belts come from). The first time I did this, I struggled for like an hour. The second time it was a minute, and the third time it was 10 seconds. But don't have that "first time experience" when you're leaving the hospital with no sleep and you're totally delirious and now need to grope around in a car.

Bouncy Seat

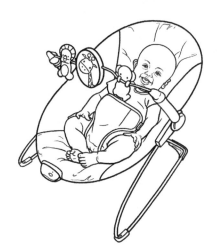

Newborns can't be left by themselves, really not even for a minute unless they're well strapped-in or somesuch... so something like this can make a tremendous difference in parents being able to do basic things like take a shower when they're home alone with baby. Or go pee while your spouse is taking out the garbage.

The company "Bright Starts" makes a bunch of stuff that's around $20-40, and we thought most of it was fantastic. Plus, it was cheap enough that we didn't feel bad when we stopped liking something and gave it away or threw it out. But this particular item, currently $28, was tremendously useful.

Boppy Pillow

It's shaped like the letter "U", and you need one. Newborns can't hold their heads up, although they do like to look around (during the few hours they're awake). But you have to be careful when they're super-tiny because they can't "roll over" yet... which means the first time they manage this trick, they can actually suffocate themselves by rolling over onto something they can't get off of. Not to scare you, but still, this is a thing.

So if you want to leave them alone for a moment, even just long enough to open a can of soup and throw it into the microwave, you still need to know that baby is "secured" somehow. The "boppy pillow" is a great solution for that.

Also, if Mommy is nursing, a newborn is too small to sit in her lap and still reach her breast... which means that Mommy's arms will get very tired - unless you have a cushion of just the right size and shape, like this one. The brand "Boppy" makes many colors, but there's one called "Leachco Cuddle-U Basic Nursing Pillow" that we especially liked.

Baby Book

People will give you these things... various versions of a diary to remember special moments (first words, learns to crawl, each month's new silly thing, first giant poo, and so on).

The thing is, you're going to be really busy in that first year. Plus deliriously tired for the first few weeks or months. Which means it's very unlikely you feel like you have "extra time" for additional "homework", no matter how charming it may be. But you *do* actually want to save these memories, to someday be able to tell your kid details of the first year. Because they *will* ask.

We highly recommend the "CR Gibson" sticker calendars as a compromise. In our house we did the "Woodland Creatures" version. Put it on your fridge or door or whatever, and there are *stickers* for the various milestones ("first eats solid food," "says mama", etc.) What could possibly be easier? Trust me, this is your **"I have zero time for this"** solution.

Check out the sticker page and think of them like game "achievements" to "unlock"... when they happen on a particular day, just put the sticker on that day. This is as close to "zero work" as you can get, which is important. Even if you think you have time to keep a "daily diary" or do some larger project, this is still a good backup plan.

Diaper Genie

Blogs like to dispute whether this is good or not, but just buy the damn thing. $35. It's plastic and clunky and poorly made... but it does the totally awesome thing of making it so you can change a diaper at 3am and go back to bed without having to take out the trash or smell poo in you house.

Just buy it. When it arrives, you'll be all "WTF, such a piece of junk"… but trust me, this is worth having. I promise, it's a small price to pay for an insurance policy against smelling poo.

Changing Table

You'll wreck your back if you don't have something around waist-height for this. You can use your dining table, in case of emergency, but I'd suggest springing for a chest of drawers that's meant for this purpose. You'll need someplace to store diapers and butt-cream, etc., anyway. And by the time your baby outgrows the need for a changing table, you'll still need a dresser for baby's clothes. $400-$1000 should give you your choice. I would suggest avoiding Ikea for this item, if you can afford to, because baby could well end up keeping this piece of furniture all the way through college age. (As long as you don't buy particleboard).

Diaper Bag

You need this. What makes it a "diaper bag" is that (a) it's big enough for diapers, and (b) it has several separate compartments - for food, diapers, wipes, changing pad, etc. Either Mommy or Daddy needs to be able to grab this at a moment's notice, or throw it into the compartment under the stroller. And you need to have confidence that it contains all the stuff you might need. (Diapers, wipes, rash cream, pacifier if you use them, bottles of formula or pouches of food.)

There are some nice ones at http://www.giggle.com/diaper-bags/, or try shopping at Target or Babies 'r' Us. Buy it before baby arrives, because *after* baby arrives, you'll discover that you literally can't leave the house without this bag. You won't be able to shop for it without risking a giant poo problem, so just get the bag before the baby arrives.

Go for basic black if you can find it, since this item is going everywhere you go, for years, and the cutesy ones with the loud patterns feel weird at grownup parties.

Changing Mat

You need this too. The nice ones have room for a few diapers and wipes. But what really matters is that you need a surface for your baby when you're changing a diaper away from home. Whether it's a friend's sofa or a gas station restroom, you don't want your baby's poopy butt touching other people's stuff. You'll see. Get the "Skip Hop" portable changing mat.

Changing Pad

This is for your house. You need something soft and easily cleaned for baby to lie on while diapers are being changed... I highly recommend the "Keekaroo Peanut Changer", even though it's expensive at $129. Some cheaper ones are uncomfortable or hard to clean, but this product is very nice.

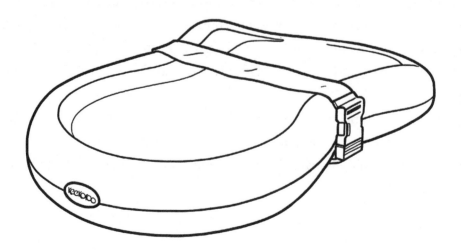

Especially great is the "seat belt" feature, which means that if you're alone and you need to reach for something while changing baby, you can strap baby down to prevent a fall. Again, trust me, this is one of the "must-have" items. If the price is really a hardship, you could use a few bath-towels, folded over enough times to make a soft 'mattress'... but this will be less work for you, plus more comfortable and sanitary for baby.

Chux

You might choose to buy these disposable mats. (For $14, it's a no-brainer that you should try a pack; if it doesn't work as part of your routine, then just don't buy more.) When you're changing the diaper, these go *under* the baby's butt. So, if poo leaks and smears (which sometimes happens), then it gets one of these pads dirty and you replace the disposable pad with a fresh one.

These pads were meant to go into cribs (or adult beds) like external diapers for bed-wetters, but they work great on the changing table. Most of the time, when you change diapers there won't be any spillage... which means each of these mats might be re-used 5-10x before you swap it out for another. But when the giant poo-splosion does happen, you'll be thanking me if one of these was there to catch it. Think about it; each one is $1 per time you don't have to scrub poo off your changing pad.

Crib

You won't need this until baby is 3 months old or so... *But* here's the thing: Furniture often takes 2-4 months to be delivered. Mommy will want to have a say in this purchase, and she will not want to waddle around a furniture store when she's 9 months pregnant. And after baby is born, you will (a) still not want to wander around a furniture store, and (b) you might need it sooner than the delivery time allows, which means you could end up settling for a crappy or overpriced item just to get a "quickship" delivery.

Unless money is super-tight, I'd suggest getting this out of the way around month 6 of pregnancy, even though that means it will arrive long before you need it. Babies-R-Us has quite a few around $200-350.

Important Feature: most of these have adjustable height. Be sure yours does too. It means that when baby is tiny, the mattress is higher up (easier for you to put baby in and out). Then, as baby grows, you can lower the mattress as necessary, to keep baby from climbing out. Have mercy on Mom: even a few months after giving birth, try not to make her bend over and lift things too much (including baby).

Receiving Blankets

People will probably give you these, but buy a few just in case. Newborns like to be "swaddled", which means "wrapped up like a tight burrito". You'll learn how to do it while you're in the hospital; make sure you get the nurses to show you how, as many times as necessary for you to feel comfortable. They're busy, so they might not *volunteer* to help teach you, (especially since they don't know whether you're clueless or not), but they will probably be very helpful if you ask directly.

At least *among* the many nurses, there should at least be *one* nice one who will help you (if not all of them). Some companies sell elaborate "form-fitting" swaddling blankets, sometimes with velcro;

I found these to be silly gimmicks. A big square of nice fabric is all you need. BTW, "swaddling blanket" = "receiving blanket"; same thing.

Onesies

People are very likely to give you a bunch of baby clothes, so I'm not even putting it on the list. For $10 you can get 5; try amazon.com or carters.com. Don't buy newborn-sized clothing that goes on "over-the-head". Look for front-snap items. As soon as your kid is less floppy, over-the-head is fine (6-12 months).

Travel Crib

We recommend the "Guava Family Lotus Everywhere Travel Crib". At $200 this is a bit pricey for a "second crib", but if you can afford it, for visits to grandparents and elsewhere, this is awesome. And as an alternative, you could even use this as the *only* crib, for quite a while.

We tried a whole bunch of brands and models. Some were too heavy, some were too difficult to cram into the carrying case, and one was rejected by my kid for who-knows-why. This one is great because it's easy to assemble, reasonable weight, well made, and has nice optional accessories (light shade, mosquito net, etc.). We love it.

Baby Bathtub

We got a stylish $100 one from Giggle, and it was overpriced bullshit. Later replaced it with a $15 ugly one, which worked great. When baby first arrives, you'll do sponge baths. Then you can use the kitchen sink. This is not an emergency item, so don't worry about it until you feel like it. While they are tiny, you can also hold baby during your own shower.

High Chair

Forget about it, this is for much later. You will have a choice of "stands by itself" or "clips onto edge of table". We found that the clippy type is sketchy. But none of this matters until baby can sit up straight, which might be around age 6-9 months - so worry about it later.

Feeding

Don't worry, your baby won't "eat you out of house and home". They're tiny, and even though they feed frequently, they don't eat very *much*. If groceries aren't currently a hardship, then don't expect baby food to be a big burden either.

Nursing

Doctors and nurses will pressure your wife to nurse your baby. (Hint: "Nursing" means "Breast-Feeding".) Be supportive of her at every stage, no matter what she wants to do, including if she changes her mind in either direction. Nursing is super-duper-healthy for the kid. Doctors and nurses will talk your ears off about this. But sometimes it just doesn't work out, which can be for many reasons. Everyone's ultra-emotional when a baby arrives.

If nursing isn't working out, it's your job to make sure your wife understands that she's not somehow failing at being a mom. She's not. She's also not failing if she simply doesn't want to do it. Let her choose this, and support the choice; it's her body and you don't know how her stuff works or feels.

If she does end up nursing, give a big hooray, and support however she feels about privacy (whether she wants to hide in a tent, or strut bare-chested down the street, or anything in between). When it comes to this part of parenting, your job is to be unconditional cheerleader for Mommy.

Formula

Even if your baby is nursing, if baby can *also* take formula, this will be easier on you and Mommy. Some babies refuse. (Some Moms refuse, for that matter.) Newborns need to eat every 2hrs or so, which means that's how often they wake up. Belly the size of a ping-pong ball. So, if you can be responsible for some of the feedings in the middle of the night, then Mommy can get 4 consecutive hours of sleep instead of 2. Which will make her less irritable.

So it will be better for *all three* of you if Daddy can bear some of the load. You can buy it "pre-mixed" in bottles, which is super-easy to deal with. The hospital will probably use Similac Infant Formula, which is fine, and Amazon will deliver it by the case. Or you can save some money by buying powder and mixing it yourself (bit of a nuisance).

Bottles

It's possible to spend a fortune on these things, especially if you get fancy sterilizers and other equipment. But here's the thing: each baby is different, and sometimes they just decide that they will or won't accept some particular product. No rhyme or reason. *And they don't care how much you spent.* You don't even know if baby is going to be nursing or not.

Even if your wife has a plan, know this: (1) people can change their minds, (2) biology might work better or worse than expected, (3) hormones can have unexpected changes in how people feel about things.) You can Amazon all this stuff, so do it after baby is born — when you see how things are going. It's not an emergency, because you don't need bottles for nursing and the hospital will probably send you home with formula that's already in disposable bottles.

Breast Pump

It's okay to giggle or freak out a bit about this one. Yes, there really is a gadget that will milk your wife like a cow. If you've seen "The Princess Bride", it looks a bit like the diabolical torture device in the Pits of Despair, used to suck the life out of the Dread Pirate Roberts.

The purpose is so that Mommy can fill a bottle and then Daddy can occasionally do one of the night feedings to let Mommy get more than 2 hours of sleep in a row once in a while. Or in case Mommy needs to work and be away from baby for more than two hours at a time. Or in case maybe Mommy would like to have an occasional glass of wine (she can "pump and dump", meaning "throw out the boozy breast milk after she has a drink").

Irrelevant if baby ends up taking only formula. These things cost like $200-300 plus accessories, and it's possible that Mom's biology won't allow for nursing. Or she may choose not to. This is not an item that people want to buy "used", so you're stuck with it once you buy one.

Mommy might choose to shop before baby is born. Let her have whatever she wants, if you can afford it. *(Stay out of her way on this one — just imagine how you'd feel if your wife were picking out a machine to be attached to your sensitive parts!)* Some are manual, some are automatic, some are more portable than others. Before buying anything, you might suggest first getting baby home from the hospital and seeing whether Mommy still wants it.

Alcohol

Talk to a doctor about alcohol consumption while breastfeeding, and work together with your wife to make a plan. The short version is, "a limited amount won't hurt the baby, especially if Mom has her glass of wine immediately *after* baby has been fed". Of course, if your baby is amenable to formula, things get more flexible for Mom. But it would be wise to come up with a plan well in advance, so that it doesn't turn into an argument at an emotional time later.

For Dad, if you're drinking while Mommy is staying sober for baby, well, then you're kinda being a jerk. Even if Mommy says it's okay. Also, I promise you, the very first time your baby looks you in the eye while you're drunk or hung over… you will feel like a complete shit. Or you should.

Day and night, your baby needs you to have your wits about you. If you're a "40-year-old Dad," like the title of this book, then you can take a break from hard partying for a few years to be there for your baby. I don't mean you have to stay bone-dry-sober, but you know damn well your days of getting butt-wasted are over. At least for a few years, until you can leave your child in the care of grandparents for a few days. But even still, you owe it to your kid not to do anything that could get yourself hurt or in trouble. So it's time to stand up here, and if you're a party animal then prepare to dial it back.

Brands

Stores

Within your budget, you'll find some favorite stores (or websites). This is important, because you'll need to buy so much stuff that you can't always take the time to shop carefully. At the high end, we were impressed with Giggle and BuyBuyBaby. They might charge 2-3x what a discount place charges, but their stuff is pretty reliably good. However, spending this much money is totally not necessary. In the more affordable range, we thing Target is fantastic.

Clothes & Linens

For clothes and linens, we like Carter's and Target ("Cat & Jack") quite a bit. Those two brands are often super-duper-cheap, and the quality is just fine. Fabrics are soft, stitching doesn't come apart, and the designs are cute. An infant "onesie" might cost $7 from one of those brands, or $50 from a fancy designer store — and the expensive one might be scratchy and uncomfortable. (Marimekko, I'm looking at you... your stuff is adorable, but OMG my kid hates it.) Spending meaningful money on baby stuff is pretty silly. Plus, remember that anything could one day get an epic flood of poo all over it; if you buy cheap items then you won't feel bad about occasionally throwing out something that's just more foul than you want to deal with.

Accessories

For accessories, we like "Skip Hop". But mostly we have little brand loyalty for this type of thing. Google stuff. Find bloggers whose perspective you agree with.

Shipping

Get Amazon Prime, if you don't have it already. Also, Amazon.com is usually around 1% cheaper than Diapers.com, which means the only "advantage" of Diapers.com is that the shipping is usually faster. But all the baby stuff has free 2-day shipping via Amazon Prime, so you don't have to plan very far ahead to always have the right stuff around.

If you're not made out of money, then get used to "cross-checking" purchases between your in-person stores and Amazon though. Sometimes online prices are way higher. They know your browsing history and zip code too, so they know which people might not notice that they occasionally pay double or triple for low-ticket household items. It adds up.

Local Stores

Don't buy stuff like diapers in small packages from the grocery or corner store (or "conistah" if you're in Bahstin). The small packages cost several times as much as buying a 1-month supply at a time. (And a month supply is around the size of a milk crate, not a truckload.)

The Hospital Trip

I always imagined careening dangerously through streets in the middle of the night, on a rainy day, running red lights, with a sweaty wife panting through breathing exercises, and maybe one or two police cars behind me with lights and sirens blaring.

What we actually did was to take a very gentle drive, with a pre-selected calming playlist. I unloaded a rolling suitcase, and we checked in at a quiet reception desk. No theatrics, and the overall experience was more like checking in to an airport for a flight that's delayed indefinitely.

Pick a Hospital Soon

It's normal to **schedule a tour**, where they'll show you around and discuss their facilities, options, etc.

Your wife's OB-GYN probably only has privileges to deliver babies at one hospital, so if she likes her doc then this might make your decision about where to go. Your wife's biggest decision will be whether doctors are present. Even if she wants to do a "natural" (no anesthetic) childbirth, or use a midwife or doula or some such, it's still highly advisable to do it in a hospital.

Some hospitals have special rooms set aside that feel more like a home than a hospital, to allow for that experience. But in the unlikely event that something goes wrong, you *definitely* want access to real doctors and real medical equipment. Your biggest financial decision may be whether to get a private room. This varies by hospital, so do a bit of research.

Suburban places are more likely to give everyone a private room, but here in Manhattan we had to pay a lot extra for it. If your wife does not get a private room, then you will probably be kicked out at nighttime, and have to return in the morning like a visitor. This will suck for you and your wife, so if you can find a way to get a private room, it's desirable. Insurance will not cover it if you choose it as an "option", but perhaps you can find a hospital that gives it to everyone.

Pick a Pediatrician, Too

Find your pediatrician well in advance also. This will not be the OB/GYN; the O.B. literally stops paying attention to the baby the moment Mommy is no longer physically connected. Hospital will probably have a separate pediatrician in the delivery room, so that at the moment of birth there is one doctor for your wife and another doctor for the baby.

You're supposed to bring baby for the first doctor visit within a couple of days of getting home from the hospital, and at that time you will be in no condition to do research or shop for things. So now's a good time to find a local doc who takes your insurance, has a nice office, etc.

You will go to this office *many* times, so try to find a doctor (or a group practice) that has people "on call 24 hours", and that is physically easy for you to get to. When baby wakes up screaming with a giant fever in the middle of the night, you (a) want a doc who will call you back at home, to save you a scary sleepwalk/drive to the emergency room, and (b) if you *do* have to "drop in" for a quick doctor visit, you don't want it to be a long trek.

Bring to Hospital

Here's the list… there's no shame in packing a small suitcase or duffle bag:

- Your wife's favorite pillow or two. Hospital pillows are terrible.
- At least one pillow and blanket for yourself; you'll be sleeping in an uncomfortable chair, possibly for a few days.
- Bring snacks, especially things that "keep", like protein/granola bars or whatever.
- Might be smart to try and bring a bunch of singles ($20 worth?) in case you have to use a vending machine late at night.
- Bring Chap Stick or Vaseline; Mommy will thank you.
- Download some movies to your phone (or tablet). Don't count on being able to stream; the Guest WiFi might be choked too slow for video. You and your wife might be there for a *long* time.
- Don't forget a charger for your phone!

Camera in Hospital

If you can manage it, you might want to bring a nice camera. Newborns change significantly, practically every single day, so you'll want to capture as much as you can. Our hospital had an "affiliated" baby photographer, who wanted $500 to snap a few pics — but if you've got a pro camera or feel like your Facebook/Instagram feeds get a lot of love, then you can probably do great by yourself.

Just be careful not to leave valuables "on display" while you're sleeping. Maybe lock into a little duffle bag? You might not be able to wear a camera strap while sleeping awkwardly in a chair. Nurses' aides have been known to snoop and steal valuables - it's rare, but if you would be devastated by the loss of your camera then take a minute to realize a hospital room isn't a bank vault. It probably doesn't have a safe like a hotel room, either. When you do the hospital tour, you might ask about whether you'll be able to secure things somewhere.

Respect your wife's privacy. Clear all photos with her before you post them!

Delivery Date

First-time babies are very often 7+ days late, especially when Mom's not in her 20s. If your due date is August 1st, for instance, don't be surprised if Mommy is asked to come to hospital on August 8th for them to induce labor. This is not a big deal; I'm just saying, when you plan your calendar you should be ready for the possibility. For some reason, doctors seem to downplay this likelihood until after you get to the hospital - and then they're all, "duh, this always happens".

Epidural

This is a personal decision for Mommy, BUT, this part is very important: if there's even the slightest chance that she's going to want anesthesia, then tell the doctors *immediately*. Or if your plan is "see how it goes, and decide later", then that's okay - but still make sure that the moment there's a *hint* of Mommy wanting anesthesia, it's time for *Daddy* to leave the room and go grab a nurse or doctor and say **"My wife wants the epidural *right now!*"**. She can't move, and might not be able to express herself very well. Doctors don't hover over you during this process (because labor lasts for hours), so your wife is counting on you personally. *This is part of your job as Dad.*

If the two of you wait too long, it will get much harder for them to administer the meds. Which means they might need to poke her with the needle extra times, especially if she flinches because she's in pain from the coming baby. Plus, remember that doctors have many patients at the same time, so if you wait until the last minute, it's possible the doctor will say, "Gee, I have three patients ahead of you, so now you need to wait your turn." Don't mess with this; if your wife is gonna get the drugs, encourage her not be a hero: just do it early on.

Learning Diapers, Swaddling, Bottle

It's okay if you never did any of these things before. (1) Diapers are easy, and infant poop is tiny. It might sound gross, but trust me: worse things come out of your own butt. (2) Newborns like to be wrapped like an egg roll and someone will show you how. (3) You stick the bottle in their mouth and they drink automatically.

Hospital nurses are awesome. They will change your baby's diaper, feed your baby, and do all kinds of stuff like that, however many times you ask. **Make sure the nurses teach you before you leave the hospital!** Ask over and over again, until you feel like a total pro. Because when you get home, there will be no more help and you'll be all "holy crap, my baby didn't come with an instruction manual!"

Weird Dots and Spots

Nobody tells you that babies often have weird stuff happen with their skin. They might suddenly be covered in red blotches like a massive rash. Or break out in what looks like a thousand tiny pimples. A lot of this stuff goes away almost instantly, like maybe in an hour or several hours. Obviously don't be shy about grabbing a nurse or doctor if you see something weird - but at the same time, there's no need to freak out unless a doctor tells you to freak out. Unless you've had a lot of friends with babies, you might have never seen this — because nobody shares pictures of the ugly stuff.

Stock Up

While you're in the hospital, they're going to give you unlimited amounts of formula bottles, nipples, diapers, and so forth. Take as much as you can. Don't be shy about filling your backpack or whatever. They're usually pretty casual about it when you're getting ready to leave, even if you say, "hey, nurse, can I have another 6-pack of formula bottles?" or whatever. This is one of the last times you'll get free stuff, so go for it and be a hoarder.

Tax, Tag, and Title

Or birth certificate and SSN, whatever.... The hospital might let you blow this off if you seem overwhelmed - but make sure you take care of it. When you're preparing to leave the hospital, or the day before, find a nurse. Make sure someone tells you what to do and gives you the paperwork to request a Birth Certificate and Social Security Number for baby. No downside, and you may as well get this task out of the way. When you get home, it will be much harder to find the time to deal with this (or anything).

Start College Savings Right Away

Set up a College Fund during baby's first month. No kidding. It's called a "529 Education Plan", and it's run through the state. I know the details for NY, but you'll have to research for your home state. It's like an IRA (retirement account), but in your kid's name. You can put money in, and control (a bit) how it's invested, but basically it just accumulates until baby is old enough for college.

If the money is ultimately spent on education, then the interest is never taxed. Even if you're short on cash right now, you can open an account with only $1 - so that at least you know it's there. Other people can make contributions, too, in your child's name. In order to set this up, you will need baby's Social Security Number and Birth Certificate, which should arrive in the mail several weeks after you leave the hospital (if you fill out all the paperwork).

Doing this will go a long way towards making you feel responsible, even if you haven't got the money to make big deposits. (Psst… and the next time you have a bit of "extra" money burning a hole in your pocket, maybe you'll think twice about who needs it more… your latest toy, or your child's future.)

First Days Home

After months of anticipation, by the end of the pregnancy you'll be eager for the baby to arrive. After many hours (possibly a few days) at the hospital, you'll be eager to get home. But once you do get home, you'll discover that things aren't quite the way you remembered.

The Good News

Newborns sleep a lot, so you'll have plenty of time to get your own sleep or talk with your wife. They love to cuddle, which can help to make you drowsy too. Cherish these moments.

The Bad News

(1) They need to be fed every two hours, day and night. (2) They can't be left alone ever. (3) Their main way of communicating is by crying, which can get on anyone's nerves - especially you've been sleep-deprived for weeks or months.

Consequences

If you're home alone with baby, and you want to go out for a slice of pizza, you need to figure out a way to bundle up your child to go as a pair. By the time baby's bundled, you'll need to change the diaper. Take off your coat. Now baby's awake and crying. Oops, hungry. Now baby's fed, so you get dressed up again. Dress baby again, oops another diaper. Finally you're both bundled up and out the door. Success?

Well, now you discover that your stroller won't fit through the door of the pizza place. Baby is sleeping so you don't want to take your child out of the bassinet stroller — walk around the block a few times. Now *you* need the bathroom, so you leave the stroller outdoors, pick up sleeping baby, go to the filthy toilet at the back of the pizza place, only to realize that peeing is a lot harder when you're holding a sleeping baby. You get the picture.

You'll manage, and you'll figure it all out... but my point is that you're about to discover that many basic things you take for granted have become a lot harder.

How to Eat

People will want to visit you to say hi to the baby and show their support for you. They will ask what they can bring. Your answer is: food! Fresh meals, preferably things that can be frozen and turn into many meals, like a whole tray of lasagna, or a spiral ham, a wheel of cheese, whatever your vices and your wife's cravings might be.

For the first few weeks, your hands will be full and basic things will be a nuisance (getting out of the house for groceries, or cooking). This is one of the nicest ways people can help. Bonus points if you can find (or pay) someone nice enough to come and clean your kitchen once or twice during those first few weeks.

How to Stay Sane

There's such a thing as a "newborn nurse". You can hire someone to come by your house and help you to take care of baby for a few hours. If you find a friendly doula or midwife in your area, they might be able to make recommendations. Or be willing to come themselves.

It could be nice to have someone watching and feeding the baby for a few hours while Mommy and Daddy get some extra sleep, or take a walk around the block to get some fresh air. Remind you how to swaddle the baby, and help you to give the newborn the first few sponge baths.

Also: there will be something like a clothespin on your baby's bellybutton (with a bit of umbilical cord), and you might be a bit squeamish about the first few sponge-baths. It's a little creepy.

I don't know if a "nurse-like person" in your area will want $20, $40, or $50/hr to come and lend a hand, or if you can afford 2hrs, 4hrs, 6hrs... but having some guidance in your own home after you get home from the hospital would be a very nice luxury — even if you only do it once or twice. Conversely, you might let your mom or mother-in-law come to stay with you for a few days if you can (and if they are willing).

We didn't think of this until it was too late, but in retrospect, it would have made those first few days at home easier.

They Sleep A Lot

FYI, newborns sleep like 16hrs/day, so you *will* have a lot of rest-time. Just not consecutively, the way you might prefer. Plus they like to sleep while lying on you or Mommy... which is charming, but impairs your ability to get stuff done. While you're figuring things out, basic activities can be pretty tough (i.e. you go out for a 20-minute errand, Mommy needs to use the bathroom but can't move without waking baby, so she has to hold it in until you get back.) Whatever logistics and sense of routine or efficiency you might have in your household, it's about to get up-ended as you re-learn to do basic things like pee.

Tons of Pictures & Videos

Use a nice camera, use your phone, use whatever. Dump them to your computer periodically. Don't worry if you haven't got time for editing pics, or choosing your favorite 10 from a batch of 1000 you snapped. Remember, digital "film" is free — but the moments will never come back, and you'll want them later.

Everything digital has a date-stamp and time-stamp, so you don't really need to "organize your pics" as you take them. But you can't go back in time and recapture a moment you missed. Of course, at the same time don't be the dick who always has a camera in his hand instead of just enjoying the moment. I dunno, find balance or something.

Daddy Pics

If you're the family photographer, you'll end up with almost zero photos of yourself with baby. We made a tradition where Mommy took a "daddy and baby" portrait every month, on the "month-day". (If your baby is born August 3rd, then for the first year you'll be celebrating the 3rd of each month. Easy to remember, it's a good time to be sure Mommy gets a pic of you with baby.)

When we reached Month 3, I had the idea to always wear the same shirt and attempt the same pose... which was kinda fun, but would have been more fun if I had the idea from the start. Whatever you do, try to make a plan from the beginning.

Same thing if Mommy is the one who always has a phone or camera out — be sure to set up a recurring plan on the calendar so you don't accidentally let a few months go by with no good pics. It's an easier mistake than you might realize.

First Date & Date Nights

Figure out who you *really, really* trust with your baby, so that you and Mommy can have a bit of alone-time. Super-important. Even if you live in different cities from your families, perhaps some grandparents will visit for a little while to help out at the beginning? An aunt or uncle? Anything to maximize your support will make you very happy. And don't schedule all your help for the same time. If there are two sets of family members who can each help for a week, have them visit on *different weeks!*

That very first "meal alone together as parents" was really special for us. And at some point early on, you'll want to set up a recurring system, to make sure you don't forget to get out of the house.

Parental Leave from Work

Arrange for Daddy to have as much as you can afford, without jeopardizing your job or taking away money for household essentials. For Daddy, I'd say that less than two weeks is insane — but if you can manage 4, 6, or 8 weeks, then you and your wife will be thrilled. When planning your work calendar, remember that if Mommy is in her late 30s or early 40s, it's not unusual for baby to be a week later than expected.

In my case, I was working as an hourly contractor for one big client at the time our child arrived, so there was no concept of "paid leave". I did arrange, however, that for two weeks that my client would literally not phone or email me. After that, I worked half-time for three months. My client at that time, often a difficult person to deal with, was surprisingly sympathetic — you may find the same, that business colleagues who are parents themselves will give you more leeway than you expect.

Everyone needs to find their own balance, but I'm confident you will enjoy however much time you can get for this. Personally, my whole adult life I aimed at spending two years unpaid leave with my child, but when baby arrived it simply wasn't something I could afford. Oh, well. Still, no reason to pout! Get as much time off as you can, enjoy it, and then get back to work.

The First Year

Many people will tell you the first year is the easiest, but during that first year this statement will seem like lunacy. Here's what they really mean: "In the first year, especially the first six months, your infant mostly sleeps and barely moves - so even though you might be confused about adapting to your new identity as a parent, there's something idyllic about the time before backtalk, negotiation over toys, questionable romances, or driving lessons."

The first year is hard because your whole life will be turned upside down. It's easy because once you figure out diapers and bottles, your baby's needs are pretty simple.

Your New Community

Find other parents of same-age kids to be friends with. Seriously. You need a support group. People to whom you can vent, and people who will share "best practices". Once you have an infant, you can go to playgrounds and chat with other people. (Most kids will be running, obviously, but there will be some parents with sleeping newborns in stroller-bassinets or carriers.)

Some neighborhoods have websites or forums or online groups you can join. In fact, sometimes they are organized by the month and year of birth, so you might be able to start *now* connecting with neighbors expecting children at the same time as you.

Don't worry, it's fine if you don't need "one more damn thing to do" right now. But it's nice to have a few local people with kids of identical age, who you can text questions to, or meet for a coffee or playground visit, or just generally vent. And if you're in your 40s then your own friends probably have older kids and won't remember the infant stuff.

Bubble

For the first three months, it's extra-serious if baby gets a bad sickness — so there's nothing wrong with being a little reclusive at first. It doesn't require "pandemic-level" isolation, but be generally careful. Besides, you'll be physically and emotionally exhausted, plus busy trying to figure things out, fix your job situation, etc.

Quiet or Loud House

Inside the womb, things are actually quite loud. (Imagine "rushing water" sounds.) So newborns are actually quite good at sleeping in a noisy setting. If you make a point of not lowering your voices and turning down the TV or music for baby's sleep-time, then you might be able to get yourself a baby that lets you live a normal life after baby's bedtime.

OTOH, if you make a point of being a super-tiptoe-quiet person, then you may end up training baby to require that (which will cramp your style later, when you'd like to watch a movie without headphones or have friends over for dinner past baby's bedtime).

It may be your instinct to tiptoe, but it's less necessary than you think. Some friends made a point of blasting music like Beastie Boys when baby was going to sleep, and it made their lives easier during the toddler years.

Social Media

Make a plan with your partner, about how much visibility you want your child to have. Some people Facebook daily pics, while others pretend online they haven't got children at all. Personally, our guideline is the "Mean Girl". Some day, there will be a "mean girl" in school with our daughter. We don't want that girl to be able to get online and find embarrassing pictures of our daughter. Or, said differently, we don't want her online until she's old enough to consent to being online. Which means "old enough to understand what that means, and its consequences".

Posting baby pics always gets a ton of "likes," but in my opinion, that would be selling out our daughter's privacy in exchange for meaningless social validation. We *occasionally* put up a single cheerful pic of our kid, so that distant friends can see her growing up... but we only do it around every six months. Remember, you can always send an email some current photos to a list of important friends or family, and that's way more private than social media.

We *never* post anything negative or embarrassing (for us that means no pics in diapers, no nudity, no pics crying, no "messy food face", etc...) We also *never* give any data about where/when our daughter will be - especially not where her daycare is (or even hints like what kind of program it is), what are our favorite restaurants to take her to, where does she like to play, or anything like that.

Not saying you should do what we do, but I am saying you should think it over and make a plan. You should know whether you're going to Facebook that first baby pic from the hospital or not. For that matter, you should know whether you want strangers on social media to know your kid's name and birth date.

Passwords

Absolutely never ever ever use your baby's name or birthdate as any part of any password for anything. Seems obvious, especially for anyone who uses technology in their daily life or career... but still it needs to be said.

Day Care

Where your child goes during the daytime (if you and your partner have jobs) will be an issue, but you'll have plenty of time to think about it. Having a child may change your views about your work life and goals, and even more so for Mommy. You both have hormone stuff going on right now, but hers is 100x more dramatic than yours. And the moment of birth triggers stuff too, so don't bother planning things just yet.

Sign Language

A little-known fact is that your baby is mentally ready to say certain words sooner than the physical ability arrives. Starting around 4-6 months, you may be able to teach your child a few words in American Sign Language. Especially common are the words for "more", "milk", "mommy" and "daddy". Maybe also "hungry", "tired", "happy", and "thank you". There's a great book called "Baby Signs", or of course you can learn from YouTube.

Pacifier

There are different schools of thought on this. Do your research and try stuff. It's not an emergency. Use the paci too much and it can cause dental trouble or delay speech development. However, thumb-sucking can do that also, and at least you can take away a pacifier more easily than you can confiscate a thumb.

Weaning

If there's nursing, then there will eventually be weaning. (The word just means "the end of nursing".) This is not an emergency for you; your wife will work it out. I'm saying this will be easy, but you have plenty of time for research and finding help.

Sleep

Newborns are naturally great at sleeping, like 16hrs/day or more. (Just not in a row, the way you'd prefer.) But they also go through many phases, some of which are really hard. It's connected with their brain development, as they gain the ability to dream and clear other neurological milestones.

If baby sleeps well for a month, and then spends a week having problems, well, sometimes stuff like that just happens. Maybe it's your fault. Too loud, too quiet, too hot, too noisy, too smelly, who knows? Or maybe it's just part of growing up. Maybe it's hunger? Or gas? Who knows? They're not good at telling you.

Expect to need to try new things often. Try different sound machines. Louder or softer. When our baby hit 3 months, our savior was the Baby Merlin's Magic Sleepsuit ($40) – keep a link to that product handy; many other parents told us the same thing. But you may need to explore stuff. When baby is newborn, you'll want baby right next to you and/or mommy.

Co-Sleeping

This term means "baby sleeps in the same bed as parents." I advise strongly against doing this. One friend told me, "If you're going to try co-sleeping, you may as well call a divorce lawyer at the same time." Let that sink in.

When you're tired, and baby won't sleep without being held, there's a temptation to just give in. But use the glider for that. Doctors will probably tell you not to sleep in bed with your infant because of the risk that one of you rolls over onto your baby and smothers the kid. Which also a possibility.

Don't start a habit of baby sleeping literally between the parents at night. Remember how that baby was made? It won't happen if baby is physically between you.

Baby might push hard for your bed to be "the only way baby can sleep", but if you acquiesce then every week or month that goes by, the baby will be more insistent. If baby is sick and having a really hard time, or if you're traveling and baby's freaked out by the unfamiliar place, then you might make an exception (although see above about suffocation fears). But definitely don't let it become a habit for baby to be in the parents' bed.

Boundaries. Super-important. If you let this bad habit start then it can continue through school-age or beyond — and I see a shocking correlation between people who have done this and also had serious trouble in their relationships.

Sleep Training – Quick Summary

There is debate about the correct age for "sleep training", whether it's 3, 4, 6, or 9 months. Here's what it's all about: Baby wants you to put baby to sleep. Baby likes to fall asleep "on you", and then you'll "trick" baby by doing a sneaky transfer into the bassinet or crib. When baby wakes up in the middle of the night, you'll get up and do this again. But there comes an age when baby has to learn that it's possible to fall asleep *without* you.

"Sleep Training" is a bit like "breaking a horse", in that you will need to defeat the will of your child. This will be very painful and difficult, and will be hard on you and your relationship. Be strong.

Because of how hormones work, this is likely to be be harder on Mommy than on Daddy, so Daddy should remember to be extra-patient no matter what gets said. Mommy should remember to lean on Daddy's strength, rather than "defending" baby. Everyone needs to have faith that their lives will be better when the parents can get more sleep... Sleep is the key to having the strength and patience to being good parents and good spouses. This is hard, but your lives will be better after.

First Birthday

Make a big fuss. No, baby will not remember. But this isn't for baby. It's for *you!* It's a celebration that you made it through the first year! Holy crap, you did it! It's also the last time you can impose on all your friends and family for gifts and celebration. (The Grandparents will like all the birthdays, and baby's Aunts and Uncles might care a bit, but don't fault your childless friends if they don't give a crap about your kid's third birthday party.)

Eventually your kid will have preferences, and school friends. Even more so if the birthday falls during the school year, and there are class parties. But for the first party, make a big deal. Let people buy you stuff and fuss over you, show up and pinch the cheeks and say, "wow, so big already!".

Let your kid ruin the chocolate cake by face-planting into the icing, and make your guests eat the drool cake anyway. You weren't able to really "celebrate" at the time baby was born, because (a) hospital, (b) no alcohol, (c) wife just got ripped apart, (d) baby shouldn't be exposed to germs anyway, etc.

Now that we live in an era where you're not supposed to have martinis and cigars in the hospital, the First Birthday is more the time for celebrating than the actual birth. *Live it up!*

Sleep Training: A Deeper Dive

Sleep Training is also known as "one terrible evening, followed by many blissful nights." Whether you choose to do it at 3, 4, 6, or 9 months, *you must do this, sooner or later. The only question is when.*

Baby is capable of waking up 5-10x each night, and parents will literally become psychotic if that continues indefinitely. Sleep Deprivation makes Mommy and Daddy shorter tempered with each other. In fact, subjecting people to constant wake-ups is considered a war crime under the Geneva Convention — and your baby will be doing it to you. (source: https://fas.org/irp/crs/RL32567.pdf)

So, when baby is old enough and parents are ready to take on a challenge, you need to choose a date together and go through this difficult process. If you let baby's first birthday come without sleep training, you may have big sleep trouble for many years to come. Don't.

Here's how the "training" works:

1) you put the baby in the crib, awake.
2) you say good night and leave the room, closing the door.
3) baby screams as if being literally torn apart by demons, for a super-long time.
4) the parents fight brutally about why the hell they're doing this.
5) the next day, Mommy + Daddy + Baby all have much better lives. Srsly.

There are three versions of Sleep Training:

"Cry It Out"

You close the baby's door, turn up the stereo, open a bottle of wine, put in earplugs, and try really hard not to think about it for an hour or two. Seems super-cruel, but it works really fast.

"Ferberizing"

Same thing, but you go in to check on baby occasionally, so baby doesn't feel abandoned. some say "every 5 minutes", or some do a fibonacci series (1, 1, 2, 3, 5, 8, 13, 21, 34 minutes), getting longer each time. Some people think this is less cruel because the baby feels less abandoned; others think it is more cruel, because it stretches out the process quite a bit.

"Cave in"

This is when you try doing Sleep Training, and then chicken out and let the child win. This is the worst thing you can do. If baby screams for 30 minutes of hyperventilating and totally freaking out, and then you come in... you have succeeded in teaching baby "any time things don't go well, don't give up, just scream for a really long time". Next time baby will scream even longer, because it worked the first time.

Whatever you do, Mommy and Daddy have to be on the same page. And support each other. And uphold the decision. *Do not* teach your baby the lesson that, "screaming for hours will eventually get what I want", because that's the kind of lesson they'll pick up *really fast*, and it will plague you long-term.

We did "CIO" at 9 months, although we considered it at 3-4 months, and we tried unsuccessfully at 6 months (caved).

There is debate about whether a 3-month old baby can hold enough food in its belly to sleep through the night without being hungry, and there's also debate about whether the neurological development is sufficient at that point. Doctors seem quite comfortable with 6 months being safe.

You cannot use this tactic if baby is older than 9 months or so. Why? Because once baby can stand and toddle around the crib, baby can keep itself awake indefinitely. Once baby hits that threshold, you're stuck. If baby hasn't learned to sleep, you may have long-term difficulties.

You cannot use this tactic if baby doesn't have a separate room with a physical door. Baby knows when parents are around, more by smell than by sound or sight. If baby's screaming while you're standing right there (or sitting on a sofa that baby can see/hear/smell), then you're not "training" anything; you're just being cruel. If your home hasn't got room for baby to be separate, then consider sleeping on the couch or an air mattress for a week or so, to facilitate this process.

The training works only if you do it while baby is so young that it's stuck lying down. Basically, baby is capable of falling asleep without you, but doesn't know it. Because baby's language skills aren't developed yet, you can't "convince" baby of this. You need baby to sleep on its own, without you, and the only way you can communicate it is to force the baby to face its fear and do it.

If you do it at bedtime, and baby is comfortable and safe, then baby will scream for a very long time but eventually pass out from exhaustion. It's a rite of passage.

In our case, the first day was maybe 90 minutes of hellish screaming. Second day was 20 minutes. Third day was 5 minutes. After that, 0-1 minutes. We have heard that this is pretty typical. I think one parent told me it was an hour for the first 3-4 days, but most say that it's basically one day of excruciating torture, then a few days of being somewhat bad, and then the struggle is over.

People will ask you if baby is "sleeping through the night yet", and this is often what they're talking about. Or maybe just asking if baby's able to go for 5-10hrs without waking you.

The good news about Sleep Training: *Once you do it, Mommy and Daddy can have 12 hours to themselves!* Baby will go to bed and stay asleep for a very long time! Enough time to clean up the house, have a nice dinner, "Netflix and Chill", and sleep a whole 8 hours totally un-interrupted. Every night.

If you travel, or if baby gets sick, it's possible you'll have to "re-do" the sleep training occasionally... but fundamentally, once you get past that *one* bad night in the beginning, the baby knows that sleep is possible. If there's a "regression" and you need to "start over", it will probably only be 10-20 minutes of crying, for a single night. Basically, once you've done this you get your life back in a *huge* way.

Other Books

You won't have time for stuff. Not now, and even less after baby is born. You need handy info sources, but you also need them to "get right to the point". Out of the mountain of books we looked at, these have been the big winners:

Reference

* **Baby Owner's Manual**: Concise and good, in an entertaining format.

* **Baby 411**: Great advice format, in that it doesn't really "take sides". Often it will present two or more contrary opinions, and explain the thinking behind each.

* **Baby Signs**: Tiny kids can learn American Sign Language before they can speak words. Even teaching just a few, like "milk" and "more" is very fun and will help you to understand your child in those early months.

* **Happiest Baby on the Block**: Really good ideas about how to have less crying. Worth the read - a happy baby is priceless!

* **The Wonder Weeks**: Developmental milestones to look for... totally fun, and many things you might not have noticed if they weren't called to your attention. A bit of a long book, but you only need to read the chapters one at a time - each chapter tells you something to watch for in your child's development. No need to read ahead; they happen in order.

Humor

* **Safe Baby Handling Tips**
* **Go The Fuck To Sleep**
* **Toddlers are Assholes**
* **Shit my Kids Ruined**

Things to Look Forward To

⭐ You will make new friends. This is likely to be the biggest new infusion into your social life since college. Seriously.

⭐ Someone will be genuinely interested in all your old stories and nonsense that no one else wants to listen to.

⭐ If you haven't been well acquainted with sunrises, you may start to enjoy them.

⭐ Fancy restaurants where you couldn't get a reservation are wide open for 5pm dinner.

⭐ You'll learn to laugh instead of cry when things get stained.

⭐ You will feel more needed than you ever have before.

⭐ Falling asleep in the rocking chair with your child sleeping on you is one of the most beautiful and comforting experiences you'll ever have.

Conclusion

Wow. You made it.

There are a thousand other issues that arise in the first year; this isn't supposed to be a comprehensive parenting guide. It's supposed to be "key learnings from a Dad in his 40s".

Many things surprised me. For some products, I had to buy 5 different versions before finding one that worked right. This book is really a collection of the "Unexpected Best Practices" or "Stuff Nobody Tells Guys Who Are Bachelors Into Their Late 30s".

This book is the list I wish I had when my wife was in her second trimester. I hope you find it useful!

— Aaron

25967785R00050